Spiritual Journey

Jessica McCormack

REJOICE
Essential Publishing

Copyright © 2020 by Jessica McCormack

All rights reserved. No part of this publication may be reproduced, distributed or transmitted in any form or by any means, including photocopying, recording, or other electronic or mechanical methods, without the prior written permission of the publisher, except in the case of brief quotations embodied in critical reviews and certain other noncommercial uses permitted by copyright law. For permission requests, write to the publisher, addressed "Attention: Permissions Coordinator," at the address below.

Jessica McCormack/Rejoice Essential Publishing
PO BOX 512
Effingham, SC 29541
www.republishing.org

Unless otherwise indicated, scriptures are taken from the King James Version.

Scripture taken from the New King James Version®. Copyright © 1982 by Thomas Nelson. Used by permission. All rights reserved.

Spiritual Journey/Jessica McCormack
ISBN-13: 978-1-952312-20-5

Library of Congress Control Number: 2020910976

Contents

FOREWORD..vii

CHAPTER ONE: Time............................ 1

CHAPTER TWO: Comfort........................4

CHAPTER THREE: Worthines.....................8

CHAPTER FOUR: Guidance.....................11

CHAPTER FIVE: Love............................14

CHAPTER SIX: Worship.......................18

CHAPTER SEVEN: Breakthrough.............22

CHAPTER EIGHT: Goodness.....................25

CHAPTER NINE: Acceptance.................28

CHAPTER TEN: Prayer..........................31

CHAPTER ELEVEN: Temptation.................34

CHAPTER TWELVE: Patience, Faith, And War.......................39

CHAPTER THIRTEEN: Under My Feet............43

CHAPTER FOURTEEN: Chaotic Faith..............47

CHAPTER FIFTEEN:	The Power of The Tongue..............51
CHAPTER SIXTEEN:	Spiritual Gifts............55
CHAPTER SEVENTEEN:	Anger..........................60
CHAPTER EIGHTEEN:	Grief............................64
CHAPTER NINETEEN:	Seeking Lost Souls............................68
CHAPTER TWENTY:	Hearing God's Voice...........................71

ABOUT THE AUTHOR..75

Foreword

"Spiritual Journey," is very inspirational. I recommend this book to everyone, babes in Christ, and the mature because it provides spiritual encouragement that will whet your spiritual appetite. "Spiritual Journey," will help you keep walking towards God on your spiritual journey.

—Bishop Ron Webb

CHAPTER ONE

Time

When you give someone your time, you are giving them a portion of your life that you'll never get back.

— Rick Warren.

First and foremost is the time we give over to God. No matter how busy our lives are or how much time simply escapes us, we must find time to pray and read His Word. It is essential to our well-being. It is the foundation on which we build our lives. I'm not sure about you, but I look forward to my time with the Lord daily. It is like meeting with your very best friend for coffee. Of course, I'm only human, so there are times when it passes me by. Life is full of distractions and it sometimes seems there is not enough time in the day. If you're like me – I have three children – between school, homework, sports, and everything in between, time often just disappears. The thing is, when I don't find time for the Lord, I physically feel it. I feel lost and uncertain of my next move. When you give God the first portion of the morning, you set the tone for the rest of the day. He is our connection to feel Heaven.

Besides time with God, it is also important to have time with family and friends. God gave each of us specific family and friends to surround us with love and happiness. God hand-picked your family, one by one. He has shown me that family comes in all forms. Not only through blood but in many different loving ways. Whether or not you're born to live with the same parents, or in half families, step-families, adoption, with church family or friends, that is what is destined to become your family. It's a body of people who come together to spend their time with one another. God blesses us with amazing people in our lives who show love, comfort, and encouragement. Love the family God gave you. Don't let relationships slip away, hold onto those who mean the most. Let all bitterness, anger, grudges, and jealousy go. These are things the devil holds over us so we can't enjoy the fullness of life given to us by our Heavenly Father. Call or text someone today, just to tell them you love and appreciate them!

PRAYER:

God, thank You for showing us that time is important in our lives. I pray we are continually reminded of Your goodness and blessings You have given us with families and friends. Help us to always show others we care by giving our love and time to them. Thank You. In the Name of Jesus, Amen.

CHAPTER TWO

Comfort

"Blessed be the God and Father of our Lord Jesus Christ, the Father of mercies and God of all comfort, who comforts us in all our tribulation, that we may be able to comfort those who are in any trouble, with the comfort with which we ourselves are comforted by God."

— 2 Corinthians 1:3:4 NKJV

We are all in need of the kind of comfort only God can bring. When we face troubled times, when we are dealing with a hurting heart, or when we feel empty, we know there is a God who is right there with open arms. We can trust and know that when we call on His name, He is in our midst.

Let's look at the story of Elijah and the Widow, in 1 Kings 17, starting at verse 8. God sent Elijah to Zarephath to visit a widow to provide him with water and food. When Elijah arrived, he found the woman standing at the gates and asked for some water, she was willing to give, but when he asked for some bread as well, she told Elijah she did not have enough to give him, as she was preparing the last meal for her and her son. She had reached the last of her flour and was ready to eat and wait to die with her son. Elijah spoke to the woman and told her not to fear, to make food for herself, her son and him too. He then gave her a Word from the Lord, "For thus says the Lord God of Israel; 'The bin of flour shall not be used up, nor shall the jar of oil run dry, until the day the Lord sends rain on the earth." She did so and the Lord fulfilled His promise. Can you imagine the level of comfort that must have come from this situation? A woman with no name, a woman who felt less important, a poor widow, mattered enough to God for Him to fulfill her needs.

In the eyes of God, all are equal. The same God who was there to comfort this woman in the Bible is the same God who is right here to comfort you and I. All we have to do is call out to Him in our time of need, and He will show up. He wraps His loving arms around us, giving us a feeling of peace and understanding that in all things, He will never leave us nor forsake us. You may be hurting today, you may find yourself with a broken heart, or you may simply need reassurance. Look to God. He is our only true source of pure love and comfort.

PRAYER:

God help us to remember You in all things and to turn to You. Thank You for the goodness and comfort You provide, the peace that surpasses all understanding, and the arms of mercy You hold open wide. Give us the strength and wisdom to know that no matter what situation we are in or facing, that we know we can call on you; we can never turn away too far that You won't be there waiting. Bless us today with the comfort that can only be found in You. In Jesus' precious holy name, Amen.

CHAPTER THREE

Worthiness

Many times in life, we feel that we are "not good enough." Sometimes, this feeling comes from abuse and being put down your whole life; sometimes, there are other underlying issues. The devil wants nothing more than to keep us down and make us feel worthless. It's a good thing we know we were created in the image of God. In Genesis 1:27, we are told that "God created man in His own image; in the image of God He created him; male and female He created them."

Spiritual Journey

Here are some things from my childhood that left me feeling that I was "not good enough." I always tried to go above and beyond everything to fulfill that emptiness. I got into some things that I knew in my heart weren't right, but I craved that sense of goodness so badly that I was willing to jeopardize my faith. Do you ever feel like no matter what you do in life, it's never good enough for someone? Do you find yourself looking for new ways to fulfill that vacuum? When we're hurting and have a sense of longing and brokenness, we tend to look beyond what we know in our hearts to be right. I wish I could go back and know what I know now. But then, I wouldn't be who I am today without having gone through some of those things.

I had to watch everyone around me receive blessing after blessing and watch their dreams coming true, while I sat back feeling empty and unworthy. I couldn't grasp what was happening or why. Why wasn't I good enough in my daily life or in the way I walked with Christ? For years, I held this over myself; I tried getting attention in every possible way. I am here to tell you there is a way out. God didn't create us to live in bondage. God showed me that in His eyes, I am good enough. If He created me in His image, how could I not be beautiful in His sight? Once I laid myself at His feet, the shadow hanging over me lifted. I realized how truly blessed I was this whole time. He is the only one who can fill the emptiness in our hearts and souls. Can you imagine having someone who takes away that constant need to impress? That feeling of emptiness and longing? Well, we can, and it is Jesus Christ. I encourage you today to give everything to Him: every hurt and every longing. Allow Him to fill the gaps.

PRAYER:

Today, Lord, I pray for my fellow brothers and sisters in Christ. When we feel unworthy, I pray You will come down and meet us where we are. I pray that You will heal broken hearts and fill in the gaps that only you can fill. Sometimes, we get off course and we need reminding who created us and that at any time, we can call on you and you will show up. Thank You, Lord, for giving us life and encouraging us to come to You as we are. In Jesus' Name, Amen.

CHAPTER FOUR

Guidance

Which of you by worrying can add one cubit to his stature? So why do you worry about clothing? Consider the lilies of the field, how they grow: they neither toil nor spin; and yet, I say to you that even Solomon in all his glory was not arrayed like one of these. Now if God so clothes the grass of the field, which today is, and tomorrow is thrown into the oven, will He not much more clothe you, O you of little faith?

— Matthew 6:27-30 NKJV

Sometimes, I get scared when I don't know what is about to happen next or how it is about to happen. I freak out. I know we should put our whole trust in God, which I do; I try. As we all know, there are also times when that's hard to do. I fear. It happens. I am human. Yet God doesn't stop moving just because I have a little fear. He still comes before me. He still moves ahead and paves the way. He still has favor for me. He still moves mountains that I otherwise wouldn't have made it past. He still gives me just enough faith to push on. He still lets me know it's ok to be scared but that I have to trust Him. He always comes through.

And the Lord, He is the One who goes before you. He will be with you, He will not leave you nor forsake you; do not fear nor be dismayed.

— Deuteronomy 31:8 NKJV

This verse tells me that He will be with me all the way and that He will never leave me. This means that even though we may be afraid of the next step in our lives or how we are going to make

Spiritual Journey

it out of a terrible situation, God is holding our hand through it all and He has already been to our destination. It's as if He goes through it all alone, moving every obstacle that may interfere, makes it to our destination, then turns back around to come and pick us up. He grabs our hand and walks us through it. That's how awesome He is — all of that love to lead the way. If you do one thing today, take time to thank God for going before you and working all things for His glory!

PRAYER:

Thank You, God, for moving mountains in our lives that would otherwise have gotten in our way. Thank You for going before us and paving a beautiful path. I know that whatever obstacle may come, You will help me through. Help me to become less fearful and more trusting of you. In Jesus' name, Amen.

CHAPTER FIVE

Love

Love suffers long and is kind; love does not envy; love does not parade itself, is not puffed up; does not behave rudely, does not seek it's own, Is not provoked, thinks no evil; does not rejoice in iniquity, but rejoices in the truth; bears all things, believes all things, hopes all things, endures all things. Love never fails. But whether there are prophecies, they will fail; whether there are tongues, they will cease; whether there is knowledge, it will vanish away.

— Corinthians 13:4-8 NKJV

Love is the greatest gift of all. God loved the world so much He gave up His only son so that we could have life. Can you imagine yourself giving up your only child – or any of them – to die? To be completely honest, I could not. I cannot fathom the thought of doing so. Think about how God felt, yet He still did that for you and I. How is that not enough to be worth serving Him? In these last days, we are to show love as God loves. We cannot be afraid to spread His word; not only that, but others must see Jesus in us. It says in John 4:17-19: "Love has been perfected among us in this; that we may have boldness in the day of judgment; because as He is, so are we in the world. There is no fear in love; but perfect love casts out fear because fear involves torment. But he who fears has not been made perfect in love. We love him because He first loved us."

We don't have time to fear what others may think, or fear the outcome. When it comes to being bold for Christ, nothing horrible can come from it. Fear is of the devil. Show the love of Christ in all you do. My favorite type of love is "agape" love. It is different from any other kind of love. It is not the love we have for brothers and sisters or our spouses. Agape is a love that encompasses commitment, grace, or an act of the will. We cannot have this type of love naturally. It can only come from the Holy Spirit. Agape love is always shown by what it does. God's love is shown most evidently at the cross. We did not deserve such a sacrifice, "but God demonstrates his own love for us in this: While we were still sinners, Christ died for us" (Romans 5:8).

Agape love is not based on feeling; rather, it is a determined act of the will, a joyful resolve to put the welfare of others above our own. Love because he first loved us. 1 Corinthians 16:14 (NKJV): Let all that you do be done with love.

PRAYER:

I pray today that every step we take is the step of the Lord. In all things help us to show agape love to those around us, even those that it is hardest to give. Continue to fill us with Your love so we can pour out into others what You pour into us. Thank you, God, for giving Your only Son and thank You, Jesus, for dying on that cross to show us what pure and true love looks like. In Jesus Name, Amen.

CHAPTER SIX

Worship

Therefore, if you will worship before me, all will be Yours.

— Luke 4:7 NKJV

The definition of worship in the Oxford English Dictionary is "to have or show a strong feeling of respect and admiration for God or a god." " Worship is a gift given by God. We should feel so thankful to have that connection with God, for us to be able to bow down and worship the one true God. Lifting our hands in reverence shows God we are surrendering all we are to Him. It is saying, "Thank you Lord." I don't know about you, but I need that moment of worship, that moment of giving myself over, laying down all I am, all I've been facing. God, in turn, pours out His spirit among all flesh.

And it shall come to pass afterward that I will pour out My Spirit on all flesh; Your sons and your daughters shall prophesy, Your old men shall dream dreams, Your young men shall see visions.

—Joel 2:28 NKJV

Worship is an expression of love for our Heavenly Father. Since worship means showing a love for something, that can also mean we can worship other things. Although terrifying, we may find ourselves worshiping other idols, such as sports figures, musicians, celebrities, anyone or anything that consumes our lives and time. We become so involved in their lives or actions that we allow it to be all we worry about or all we pay attention to. We are all guilty of this, perhaps especially in the world of social media: What's the next big thing? What else can I occupy my time with? The thing is, sometimes God finds ways to remove those things from your life, even those people, at times, to show you we are to have no other gods or idols before Him.

You shall have no other gods before me.

—Exodus 20:3 NKJV

This reminds me of the story in the Bible about Hannah. She was a barren woman. Back then, a woman who couldn't bear children was shunned. Others would say horrible things to her and about her, for this very reason. Hannah did not understand why she was unable to have children. "And she was in bitterness of soul, and prayed to the Lord and wept in anguish" (Samuel 1:10). At the temple, this was her battle cry. She gave her entire heart to the Lord because she didn't know what else to do. This is what we do when we worship with our Savior. The Priest prayed over her as she was worshipping the Lord. That next morning, Hannah and her husband woke up and began to worship God. "Then they rose early in the morning and worshipped before the Lord, and returned and came to their house at Ramah. And Elkanah knew Hannah his wife, and the Lord remembered her." (1 Samuel 1:19)

Hannah knew she had to reach out in worship to our King of Kings for a miracle, and in time, she received it. Do you find yourself giving your worship to something or someone else in your life? If so, I am so thankful we have a God to turn to and say, "Lord help me to focus more on You and not this object or person. Help me to stay focused on You and take away my desires to put this thing above You."

PRAYER:

Lord, today, touch our hearts with Your presence. Give us a heart of worship. Help us to long for You and the goodness You provide. Give us the urgency to lift our hands and submit ourselves to You and only You. Thank You in Your name Jesus, Amen.

CHAPTER SEVEN

Breakthrough

We all strive to live like Christ, yet we all are sinners. I daily repent for my wrongdoings. I try not to live in sin, thinking, "Oh, I'll just repent and everything will be fine". Yes, sometimes, we mess up, but we repent and move forward; we don't keep going back.

I've had my own struggles, my own demons. I was "tied up" for years, so to speak. I fought continually to break free, but I kept falling back into the same traps. Know why? God had to show me that there is a difference in praying for freedom and praying for freedom. Confused? Let me explain, praying for freedom, sometimes, we ask God to take whatever it is away. We say, "What's wrong with me?, I know this isn't right, God, so please get this away from me." Then, we get up the next day and ask ourselves: What is one more day in sin? I'll repent later. Then the next day, we do the same. And the next.

Now praying for freedom is deciding that you will no longer live this way. Once your mind is set, enough is enough. It's getting down on your knees, day and night, begging God and rebuking your demons. It's fighting for your life, and pleading with God to do what only He can do. It's sacrificing yourself unto Him, saying: here I am, all of me. Wholeheartedly giving yourself and surrendering to the One who sets us free. It's tearing down walls and breaking chains. It is proving the only way you will look back is only to say this is where God has brought me from. Showing the enemy you are no longer captive. I am a child of God!! Set your mind and heart on the things above. Allow God to break you down to lift you back up and transform your soul.

The day I made this decision was the best day of my life. I now know what true freedom is, and you can too. God is capable of picking up the worst in us and making us whole. When temptations come my way, He is the only way I choose. What will you choose today?

PRAYER:

We are coming to You today, Lord, asking if there is anything in our hearts that can set us free. Break us down so we can return filled with You and not things of this world. Surround us with Your presence wherever we may be and in whatever situation we are dealing with. Show us Your way Lord and help us to stay on your path. Thank you, Jesus. In your Name, Amen.

CHAPTER EIGHT

Goodness

It is important for us to share great experiences with other people. This means sharing blessings and the greatness of God. I have to share the goodness of God in my life.

My whole life, I have dealt with a lot of things that some family members aren't even aware of. I will not go into detail; however, I will say these things caused some major depression in my life at a very young age. The devil has always had it in for me; it seems. He's tried taking my life in more ways than one. Depression arrived in my adult life and became second nature. Something that comes and goes. The depths became so great that they almost overtook me several times. The devil knew that if he couldn't get me any other way that he could succeed through depression. For over 20 years, it ruined many things in my life, things I can't take back. It almost ruined my marriage; it almost affected my children and almost took my life.

Several times, I told myself, "I've had enough and that I wouldn't fall into it again." The last time it stuck for me. I felt a freedom I've never felt before, like a weight being lifted and pulled away. My whole demeanor had changed. I started to feel a happiness I had never felt. When people started noticing the change in me, I had to tell them it was my God – because of Him, I could finally "breathe." God taught me how to "let go," "love myself," "forgive," and "love purely."

In our lifetimes, we all have our own demons to deal with. We battle certain struggles and feel as though we will never escape them. Sometimes, it takes a real shaking from God. Sometimes, we descend into our lowest valley, only for God to bring us back, refreshed, and stronger than ever before. If you're feeling a heaviness, or like you're stuck in a place of dryness, ask God to remove it. Take a look at yourself and your life and ask yourself if there is anything unclean you need God to remove, to open a path for blessings.

PRAYER:

God, we come to You today, some of us broken or bogged down with the things of this world. We are asking that you free us of the bondage we feel today, fill us so full of Your love that there is no room for anything else. Thank You, Lord, for promising to never leave us nor forsake us, we know that through You, anything is impossible. That includes our breakthroughs. Thank You, in Your precious name, Jesus, Amen.

CHAPTER NINE

Acceptance

Have you ever had to forgive someone who wasn't sorry? They either don't see anything wrong with their actions or they won't admit to doing wrong. It's challenging. Your flesh wants to remind them of this and get answers, closure; but in spirit, we know we need to forgive and move on. Most of the time, this person doesn't even know anything is wrong. So you ask yourself: Why? Why does this bother me so much? Well, we're only human and we tend to hold onto things that may have an effect on our present time or our future. We could always try to get answers, bring up old dirt, hurt feelings, and old wounds, but we must also learn that in order to have a pure heart before God, we have to let it go. I knew I had to let go of what had been hurting me deep inside, things I was harboring for years. That is no way to live our lives. In order to be a better person, daughter, sister, wife, and mother, I had to decide that what happened back then wasn't going to define who I am today. I couldn't let it affect my present.

We have to understand that as much as some things hurt, we have to have a clean heart before God. We must give Him every situation, good and bad. That includes letting go of hurt, pain, heartache, and any baggage we may be holding onto. Allow God to mend, restore, and make whole everything inside of you. It starts with you; God doesn't say we have to be best friends with those who damage us, but we should have a forgiving heart. Just as God has forgiven us, over and over. Make the decision today to become the best version of you!

PRAYER:

God, today I ask that if anyone reading this has a broken heart, or is holding onto some kind of hurt from their past that You take hold of the situation. Fill them with love and peace that can only come from You. Take charge of the situation that holds them captive; set them free. Give them the strength and courage to decide today to give it all to You and to let go. Going back won't change the past, help them to control their future. Give them a pure heart and a clear mind: a heart of forgiveness. Thank you, Lord. In your name, Jesus, Amen.

CHAPTER TEN

Prayer

Prayer is life changing. It's what connects us to our Heavenly Father. It's where we find our peace. When we pray, things begin to happen in our lives; situations begin to shift and the atmosphere changes. Prayer is inviting God into our lives and giving Him the ability to take over. Oftentimes, the enemy will try to defeat your prayer life. When we sit down or take time to pray, everything goes through our minds besides our prayer. What am I gonna eat for lunch? Did I give my kids enough attention last night?

What am I gonna wear tomorrow? Did I pay that bill? Your phone starts buzzing or the kids walk in. Everything possible distracts us, but when we fight through those distractions and press forward, we really encounter a breakthrough in prayer.

Do not get discouraged in your prayer life. I know that is easier said than done at times. Sometimes, we don't even have to say a word and God already knows what we're thinking, right? Just sitting in silence and allowing God to move within us is just as effective. He doesn't expect us to always have the words. He does, however, expect us to give Him our time. We find ourselves being too busy, at times, to pray. We always have an excuse, until we really need God. God did not put you off when He died for you. Matter of fact, He did it all for you and I. We owe Him our life. I love my prayer time. I get to connect with my Savior, my Father in Heaven, my Comforter, my Peacemaker, my best friend. You can literally talk to Him like you're talking to a friend. He already knows our hearts, our deepest desires. Allow God into your life, make time for Him. Be consistent in your prayer life and I promise you that you will start to see miracles happen, lives change, and your relationship with God will become clearer and more heartfelt.

PRAYER:

God, I pray today that, even in the midst of chaos, we stop and make time to pray; when things seem too distracting, I pray that we can shut them out and focus on You. I pray we continue to have that urgency to talk to you, give You our life struggles, and share our happiness with You. I pray when we feel our prayers are not being answered, that you provide us with the understanding that it may not be Your will, or maybe just not the right time. Let all things be done in due time, Lord. Thank you. In Your name Jesus, Amen.

CHAPTER ELEVEN

Temptation

No temptation has overtaken you except such as is common to man; but God is faithful, who will not allow you to be tempted beyond what you are able, but with the temptation will also make the way of escape, that you may be able to bear it.

—1 Corinthians 10:13 NKJV

Several stories in the Bible portray temptation. Let's start with the one we all know pretty well: Adam and Eve in the Garden of Eden. God specifically told them they could eat the fruit but not to eat the fruit from the tree in the middle of the garden. However, a serpent appeared to "tempt" Eve to eat an apple. He began asking questions like, "Has God indeed said, You shall not eat of every tree of the garden?" Eve reassured the serpent that God let them eat from every tree, except the one the serpent wanted her to eat from.

Let's look at this for a moment. The serpent heard Eve say she was told not to eat of that specific tree, but she could eat from any other one; and yet, he wants her to eat of this tree anyways. That's exactly how temptation works, something we know we shouldn't do, yet at that moment, it looks so good, or sounds so amazing. Sometimes, we forget to look at the future of the choice we are about to make, and we instead look to the moment and what feels the best at that specific moment. The serpent began to tell Eve she wouldn't die from eating from this tree, but that she would, in fact, become like God, knowing all. This sounded so unbelievably amazing to Eve that she caved in, she took a bite of the apple and not only did she sin, she shared that sin with Adam.

Once they both ate the fruit, they immediately had their eyes opened to their surroundings and knew they both were naked. God was not pleased with their choices. He questioned their very act, and he cursed Man and Woman for all their days.

Adam and Eve, so to speak, ruined it for the rest of us. This specific event laid out the rules for all of humanity. Their choice to give in to temptation had a huge consequence for us all. Sometimes, I think we forget how damaging giving into temptation can be. Not only do we end up with consequences for our actions, but we often hurt other people as well. If only we could always turn the other cheek, but unfortunately, we are all guilty of falling into this trap once or twice. Matthew 6:13 says, "And do not lead us into temptation; But deliver us from the evil one. For Yours is the Kingdom and the power and the glory forever. Amen." This is our prayer to our Heavenly Father to give us the strength to continue on the right path, to flee from temptation. We don't have to just sit around and wait for the temptation to come; we should be praying daily for God to open our eyes to recognize when temptation comes our way.

Let no one say when he is tempted, "I am tempted by God", for God cannot be tempted by evil, nor does He Himself tempt anyone. But each one is tempted when he is drawn away by his own desires and enticed.

James 1:13-14 NKJV

I have seen a lot of people, even myself in the midst of a terrible situation, look to God and say, "Why is this happening to me?" But it is not God who placed you there. It was the consequence of your choices that landed you there. It may not be immediate, but our sins always are made known; they will be brought to light one way or another. We don't have to give in to temptation. At that moment, we can take time to stop dead in our tracks and say, "God help me to make the best decision at this moment that is going to glorify you."

Prayer: God, I pray that when we are faced with temptation, You allow the conviction to feel so strong that we have no choice but to walk away. Never let the conviction leave us, for without it, we are truly in trouble. I pray for strength for everyone reading this today, Father, that You deliver us from evil. Make our paths straight and when temptation comes our way, we block it with prayer and fasting. Thank You for Your goodness. In Jesus' name, Amen.

CHAPTER TWELVE

Patience, Faith and War

Let's be honest, most of us don't fare well when it comes to patience. I certainly don't. When I want or need something, I want it now. Sometimes, I get it right away; sometimes, I don't. When talking patience with God, it's a fine line. I've prayed for patience before and then wondered why I bothered. You pray for patience and it's as if all Hell breaks loose. Everything that can go wrong does. So not only do we lose patience, we add a dose of anger. We find ourselves blaming God, at times. Maybe even a lot of the time. I end up feeling defeated.

Knowing that the testing of your faith produces patience.

— James 1:3 (NKJV)

That you do not become sluggish, but imitate those who through faith and patience inherit the promises.

—Hebrews 6:12 (NKJV)

As difficult as it may be at times, I have to read these Scriptures and studied their meaning. When we have faith, things begin to happen. The more we pray and read, the more our faith gets boosted, and therefore, the more patience we attain. Also, in all honesty, when we get closer to God, the more we have to face. That's because the enemy wants nothing more than to destroy your relationship with God. It is definitely a constant fight, but ask yourself: Is it worse than what Jesus went through for you? No. So I want to inherit the promises God has for me. Therefore, my faith and patience are a constant reminder of who I want to be for Christ.

Work harder, pray harder, fight like your life depends on it, because it does. We may not always get what we pray for when we want it, but that's because God's timing has its own rhythm. He usually has something better planned than what we prayed for in the first place. Just have faith that all things work for the good of those who love the Lord. He will move.

PRAYER:

Today, I pray for those of You that have a situation that seems impossible, that You give it to God in its entirety and trust Him to take control. I pray He gives you the faith to know that if you ask anything in His name that you also believe in what you're asking for. I pray you have the patience to wait, even if waiting doesn't seem to be an option, you'll just have to wait some more. I pray you open your minds and hearts to receive whatever lesson He may be showing you and learn from it. I pray that whatever isn't meant to be, that God allows it to fall away and move on your behalf. Thank you, Lord, for trusting us to go to War for You, thank You for Your blessings and lessons. We trust You in all things. In Your Name Jesus, Amen.

CHAPTER THIRTEEN

Under My Feet

And he put all things under His feet, and gave Him to be head over all things to the church, which is His body, the fullness of Him who fills all in all.

— Ephesians 1:22-23 NKJV

We read Scriptures and we sing these songs declaring that the enemy is under our feet, but do we really grasp what this means? I will tell you what it means. It means we have the authority to tread over demonic forces, over anything or situation that comes up against us. We don't have to accept the lies, the heartache, the disappointment, the fears, or anything else that may be holding us back.

Have you ever been in a situation where it feels like the enemy is tearing you down every way you turn? I know I have, and it made me so grateful to have a God that loves us; that He loves us so much as to give us the power through His name to take the enemy down. We allow ourselves to feel so discouraged and that there is nothing we can do, but we just have to wake ourselves up sometimes and say, "I got this!"

Failures in life can also hurt. They can break us down and keep us from moving forward. We have the authority to stamp on the mistakes we've made. We can step over our failures and arise victorious! We can worry, get depressed, and fill our minds with negative thoughts, or we can stand up and stride over every battle, every obstacle, every bad report, every financial situation, and every evil force that comes up against us. The enemy is under our feet through the authority of Jesus

Christ, and we can stomp our way through to victory today! Let's keep the enemy under our feet. Don't allow the enemy to destroy what God has in store for you.

In my lifetime, I have made many mistakes, but I had to learn to not dwell in the choices I made. I felt like no matter what I did in that area to fix things, I would fail in another area. The devil had me bound thinking I couldn't do good and I couldn't succeed at anything. He wanted me to feel like a failure. I had to choose to rise up and fight, stand my ground, and prove to the devil I will win.

PRAYER:

Lord, we come to You today, asking for the strength and power in Your name to fight the enemy. That no matter what happens, we stand firm in the knowledge that with You, all things are possible. We know through the blood of the lamb and the Word of Your testimony that we can fight evil, we can tear it down. Thank You for loving us that much, that we can do these things. Help us to always remember in the bad times that we don't have to accept what is going on around us, that we can break down the enemy. Thank You, Lord, Amen.

CHAPTER FOURTEEN

Chaotic Faith

For a moment now, I am going to show my vulnerability and share a part of my story where my life felt as if it was over. I had many decisions to make. I could either let the enemy steal my joy and dictate my future; or, I could take power over my thoughts and allow God to be the key to my future. My husband and I separated, life got in the way, and we lost track of why we were even together in the first place. At the time, we had two very young children. They didn't know much, but they knew daddy's house came every other weekend. They never said much, just went with the flow. Life on the outside could seem okay. However, on the inside, I reached a point where I felt like I was dying. Negativity started to creep in.

Depression has always been something I have had to deal with, and at this time, I fell hard. My heart had a huge hole that felt so heavy and empty. Things were way more complicated than just getting back together. Some things needed to change in a big way. My heart was a big part of what needed to be different. In the middle of the chaos, the confusion, the hurt, I had to stop. I had to take a break and ask myself, out of all the prayers prayed and the begging to God, why I had not just asked God to change me, if nothing else, change my heart. I needed Him to soften my heart, fill me with much more love, and help me to see the good from this. I had to create a positive mind.

When facing trials, we forget we have more control than we believe we do. We have power over our minds to allow God to pour out positivity instead of dwelling on the negative. We often want to keep blaming everyone else for the way things go or the way they end up, and often, we do not look at ourselves in the mirror. This reflection could change a lot of things.

I know my God, and I knew He was a God of healing, mending, and restoration. Little did I know, God had big plans for my husband and I. After much time apart, with healing going on in my own heart, we decided to give it another go. God not only ripped me from the inside out, took me to rock bottom, to bring me out on top, but he also softened my husband's heart. He broke us down individually, only to build us back up, better and stronger together. Faith. Without faith, we have nothing to hold onto sometimes.

Faith got me through the hardest times. Faith that no matter the circumstances, I knew God had control. No one can ever tell me that their marriage is to messed up or lost for God not to able to pick up and restore. If there are two hearts who love each other and allow God complete access, He will do it! Our love is stronger than it has ever been. We are a power couple that the enemy fears. We know our God is full of mercy and miracles, and I know He can do the same for you. We must refuse to let the enemy dictate our future. Stand your ground today and fight just as God intended. He already won the battle for us. We need only to obey.

PRAYER:

Lord, today, if anyone is hurting, broken, and they feel like life cannot go on, I ask that You give them peace and hope. If their marriage is falling apart and broken, I ask that You open their eyes to look inside themselves and be humble enough to change them if that's what is needed. I ask that You restore their love, give them encouragement, and remind them why they are together. God, with Your love and mending, I know marriages can come out better than before, just like mine did. Thank You for giving me back my other half and restoring what was once lost. I know You can and will heal others, and I am excited about that. We love You, Lord, and thank You for who You are. In your Name, Jesus, Amen.

CHAPTEEN FIFTEEN

The Power of the Tongue

Death and life are in the power of the tongue,
And those who love it will eat its fruit.

— Proverbs 18:21 NKJV

Everything we speak has power. We can choose to speak good or speak evil, but whichever we choose will have power over us. "The tongue of the wise uses knowledge rightly, But the mouth of fools pours forth foolishness." (Proverbs 15:2) Do we want our words to be used for righteous things or foolish things? In times of anger, it is easy for us to say horrible things about someone, or even about ourselves. If we only had someone to slap us and say, "Hey! Is that really gonna help if you say that? Would you say it in front of Jesus? Is it life-affirming? Anything to get us to check ourselves before it actually comes out.

I asked my 9 year old son, "When I say we have power over our tongue, what does that mean to you?," He said, "If you speak bad things, you can speak death onto someone or sickness, or you can choose to speak truth into existence." Wow. How true are those words? "For assuredly I say to you, whoever says to this mountain, 'Be removed and be cast into the sea;' and does not doubt in his heart, but believes that those things he says will be done, he will have whatever he says. Therefore I say to you whatever things you ask when you pray, believe that you receive them, and you will have them." (Mark 11:23-24) Some people find it silly to pray over every little thing, but I always tell them that we are children of the King, and he loves us so much that he wants us to have

Spiritual Journey

our hearts' desires. Choose to speak life into the things you want, and you will start to see a difference in your life and those around you. Say kind things, encourage one another, lift people up, and don't tear them down.

"I still have many things to say to you, but you cannot bear them now. However when He, the Spirit of truth has come, He will guide you into all truth; for He will not speak on His own authority, but whatever He hears He will speak; and He will tell you things to come." (John 16:12-13) It is so important we seek God to find the right words to speak. He will guide us into knowing what to say and when. It is way better than speaking and having horrible things coming out or even lies that we feel to be true. Seek God in all you do, and that includes the words coming from your mouth.

PRAYER:

Lord, today, I ask that You touch each and every individual. Give us the wisdom to know the difference in speaking life or death. Give us the discernment to evaluate our words before we speak. We want to speak good things to others and not to tear others down. Thank You for offering us the opportunity to reach out to You in all times of need. We thank You, Lord. In your name, Jesus, Amen.

CHAPTER SIXTEEN

Spiritual Gifts

There are diversities of gifts, but the same Spirit. There are differences of ministries, but the same Lord. And there are diversities of activities, but it is the same God who works all in all. But the manifestation of the Spirit is given to each one for the profit of all: for to one is given the word of wisdom through the Spirit, to another the word of knowledge through the same Spirit, to another faith by the same Spirit, to another gifts of healings by the same Spirit, to another the working of miracles, to another prophecy, to another discerning of spirits, to another different kinds of tongues, to another the interpretation of tongues. But one and the same Spirit works all these things, distributing to each one individually as He wills.

—1 Corinthians 12:4-12 NKJV

As children of God, He blesses us with spiritual gifts. We all are unique in His eyes, and He gives different gifts to us all. It is vital we seek God for the gifts that He wants us to have. We should pray for God to use us any way He would like. It is our calling He brings to our lives, which we live out for His Glory. The five ministry gifts He provides, which some call "The 5-Fold Ministry" are: Apostles, Prophets, Evangelists, Pastors, and Teachers. Each one of these is a special gift from our Heavenly Father. These gifts pour into other people in some form, whether through preaching or teaching, speaking things into their life or helping them through their lives. God speaks into you and allows you to be used by Him to voice

His word among others. If you have one of these gifts, it is a true blessing from God, as all gifts are.

God also provides us with gifts of the Holy Spirit. These include: wisdom, speaking in tongues, and interpretation of tongues, just to name a few. These are examples of how God works through us, giving us wisdom and the ability to speak in a language only He can understand. To have that connection straight to Heaven that only He holds is such a miraculous gift. When we receive the gift of speaking in tongues, we can reach Heaven and know that no one can interfere with those words and prevent them from reaching God. It is so important in our Christian path with the Lord that we pray for certain gifts and ask the Lord what He will have of us. We should all strive to be like Christ every single day and want to do His work in our lives.

In my personal experience, God has blessed me with many gifts. To name a few: ministry, discernment, and motivational gifts such as encouraging with wisdom. There were times God placed my husband and I in ministry to teach others, children, and teens. I would be lying if I said it was always smooth sailing. We had difficult moments where I wanted to give up or felt I was not good enough to fulfill that ministry. But that is what the devil wants us to feel, defeated. God places us in situations and callings that challenge us, but He will never put more on us than we can bare. He gave us the knowledge, wisdom, and encouragement we needed to go forward in those ministries. In moments I felt torn down, He uplifted me in many ways, sending me love from someone or showing me how important our ministry was. It was then I was reminded of why we were teaching in the first place. I say this to tell you, we may not always feel we are educated or worthy enough to fulfill the gift God chooses to give us, but if God gives you the ability and the open door, He will provide the rest. Trust the process.

PRAYER:

God, show up and show off in our lives. Show us what gifts You have for our lives and give us the ability to bring them forth. We pray for the knowledge and wisdom to be used by You. We pray You continue to use us and help us to know that having such gifts is beyond a blessing; that we should continue to strive for this, day in and day out. We thank You so much for loving us enough to share these gifts with us and thank You for giving us the wisdom to bring forth every word You speak through us. In your name, Jesus. Amen.

CHAPTEER SEVENTEEN

Anger

Be angry, and do not sin; do not let the sun go down on your wrath,

— Ephesians 4:26 NKJV

This Scripture tells us that before the sun goes down, we are to put away our anger. I know in my experience with anger, I suffer sometimes. It is human nature to get angry and often times it continues through to bedtime. Sometimes, I don't want to fix things; I want to be angry. I feel

I am justified in my anger. Although at times I may be, I still have to follow God's word. I have a hard time knowing that, and then actually following through. We fight with our spouse, children, family, friends, and many different people in many different ways. Being angry is not a good feeling. It leaves us feeling hurt, fed up, feelings that are not of God. I do not know about you, but I only want feelings of happiness, peace, and joy in my heart. It is in our nature to get angry, and it is going to happen over and over, but we do not have to stay with this emotion. We must make a choice not to dwell on anger. God wants us to fix it. Sometimes we must make it right even when it is not our fault.

I have been faced with many occasions where someone has angered me, and that feeling seemed to last forever. It is a bad sign when we go to sleep angry or know we made another person angry. We should want to make it right because that's what God wants us to do. My entire life, I have usually been the one who ends up going to that person to make it right. I get convicted, just as we are supposed to. Even when it was the other person's fault, I still chose to make it right, and I still do. It is a rare thing for others to come to me, but it's okay if it's always you because you're choosing to follow Jesus. We cannot let anger stop us from reaching Heaven. We are to empty ourselves of anything unclean, and that's exactly what anger is – ugly. I want so badly sometimes to bathe in my anger. I feel I have a right to be angry, and maybe I do, or maybe it's just something petty. I have to stop myself and think, "Is this how God expects me to act?"

Often, other people do not care that they made you angry, or they don't care that they feel angry, and that is not of God. Even if the other is full of anger, pettiness, or malice, you should choose to do the right thing. God will bless you for your good works. Show His love in all you do. "Blessed are the peacemakers, For they shall be called sons of God." (Matthew 5:9)

Prayer:

Lord, help us today to have a clear conscience. Let all we do be done in love and not anger. Give us the clarity and peace to push through the anger and let go of what is holding us back. Thank

You for the peace and wisdom You provide for us, allowing us to choose to do the right thing. We know anger is ugly and it is not of You, I want no part of anything that You're not a part of. We love You, Jesus. In Your name. Amen.

CHAPTEEN EIGHTEEN

Grief

And God will wipe away every tear from their eyes, there shall be no more death, nor sorrow, nor crying. There shall be no more pain, for the former things have passed away.

— Revelation 21:4 NKJV

The Lord is near to those who have a broken heart, And saves such as have contrite spirit.

— Psalms 34:18 NKJV

That means God is near to those who are hurting and crushed in spirit. Life sometimes throws us curve balls. We go through things we never thought we would have to. We face defeat. We lose loved ones or end relationships of all kinds. No matter what the case may be, we all grieve at times, and we all grieve differently. There are many forms of grief, and we do not all deal with things the same. Some people deal with grief through anger; they turn to anger and stay there. They are mad at the world and blame God or everyone else. They have a hard time facing the truth of what may have happened. It is so hard because often we do not understand why something happened and perhaps we will never.

Other times, we understand why, but we choose not to focus on it, we want to stay mad. Another response is denial; we choose to believe it did not happen. We live our lives telling ourselves it isn't true and the pain isn't real. We have delayed grief – at the moment, we choose to say we are fine and that we will get by. Then days later or sometimes years later, reality hits us hard. This is the most heartbreaking way of processing grief to my mind. It breaks my heart to see others in so much pain and yet unable to truly feel their pain. You know in your heart they're hurting so much that they just don't know how to face it or comprehend it at that moment. Do we ever really comprehend such loss?

Another response happens when reality hits right away and we don't know how to function. We have a hard time with normal daily life and routine. We feel as if we cannot face our next move or the next day: that feeling of not wanting to live any longer or wondering how we can live another day. These are times when it's important to turn to the only One who can help us move on. It doesn't mean we forget that person or that loss, but it means we can turn to the peace and comfort of our Heavenly Father. "Blessed are those who mourn, For they shall be comforted." (Matthew 5:4) God promises to be our comforter. That alone brings so much peace. I am not saying it is easy, but it is easier. I have faced loss several times in my life, and losing those we love is the hardest thing one can process. The sadness never goes away. The hurt doesn't just leave; it'll always be there in our memories, but God is the provider of comfort in times of trouble. He didn't promise life would be easy, but He did promise that He would never leave us through it. No matter what one may be facing today, give your all to Him. Allow God to wrap His loving arms around You and bring You into Him. We cannot make it through without Him.

PRAYER:

God, for those hurting today, I ask that You to bring them a peace that passes all understanding. I ask that You give them comfort in knowing You make all things new. Thank You for providing us with a pathway to reach You whenever we need You. Give encouragement to those who need comfort. Send others into their lives. Thank You for the many ways You provide all of our needs. In Jesus' name, Amen.

CHAPTER NINETEEN

Seeking Lost Souls

What better Scripture to start this out with than Luke 15:4, "What man of you, having a hundred sheep, if he loses one of them, does not leave the ninety-nine in the wilderness, and go after the one which is lost until he finds it?" This is what God does for us. He fought for us from the very beginning of time. He wants nothing more than for us to turn to Him; salvation is what He seeks. God gives us the ability to go after His sheep. He wants us to share His word and His faithfulness. We are to go out and find the one who has lost their way and bring them to Christ. As believers, we should want to share the goodness of our Lord. We should want everyone to celebrate in Heaven.

There are various ways we can seek lost souls. We do so by using the gifts God has given us, through preaching, singing, drama, or just in conversation. In all you do, acknowledge Him and His righteousness. Share the love of God with everyone around you, even if at first they don't seem interested, you are still planting that seed in their hearts. We do not go out to find God. He finds us. He may use many ways to get your attention through various events in your life or sending someone into your life to speak life into you. Personally, I love sharing my faith with others. Always back yourself up with Scripture and pray for discernment in the words you speak; that they are truth and life.

It is important to hear the words from someone, "Because of you, I didn't give up", "Because you reached out to me, I came to the Lord". Being the reason someone reaches salvation is the best gift. I want God to use me in every way possible to reach souls for His Kingdom. I am sure you want the same. For some people, shyness gets in the way or the ability to find the right words. This used to be the case for me until I prayed continually for boldness. I didn't want to hold back any longer what I was experiencing through Christ. I felt I was being selfish keeping it all to myself. Share people. Show others how good God is by telling of your testimony and where God brought you from. I get excited to listen to others speak of where they came from and how God transformed their lives and saved them from a life of Hell and torment. That's my God!!

PRAYER:

Today, I pray for boldness for others to reach sinners. Give them the words to speak up and to be used by You. When we pray and ask for guidance, I know You are there and will provide us with the wisdom of Your word to be used for Your glory. Thank You in advance for all the souls that will be saved through our obedience. In Your name, Jesus, Amen.

CHAPTER TWENTY

Hearing God's Voice

I used to think that in order to hear God's voice, I physically had to hear a voice. I heard people say things like, "God spoke to me and said...," and I remember feeling let down like God didn't want to speak to me. Now, God would show me things, open my eyes to certain circumstances or reveal things in a dream, but I knew I never heard a deep voice in my head actually speaking. My mind would fill with torment wondering why and begging God to let me hear Him. I would quote to God, "You said ask anything in Your name and it shall be given to you, so why doesn't that apply to me?"

"Whoever is of God hears the words of God. The reason why you do not hear them is that you are not of God." (John 8:47) Ouch. That Scripture right there is hurtful, yet enlightening. I am just going to be real and say, I had some things in my life that I wouldn't let go of. I lived right to the best of my ability, but there were some things which were not of God in my life. How can we expect to hear from our precious Father – such a gift – if we are not fully of Him? I had to repent of some things and surrender my whole being. It was then that I started to have those amazing encounters with God that I often dreamt of. I also learned through my process and testimony that you didn't have to "physically" hear a deep voice for God to speak to you. Sometimes, it can be hard to explain to someone just as it was for others to explain to me. It is like a conversation with a best friend. I find myself going back and forth with Him at times, questioning His words, or asking for reassurance. God will always give you confirmation, seek it.

Hearing from the Lord is such an amazing feeling. It softens our hearts and makes us vulnerable unto Him. It puts you in a spirit of reverence and surrounds you in His presence. Spend time with God, pour your heart out to Him. He hears you; He hears our every cry, our every success; He hears it all and wants nothing more than to share it with you. Did you know He longs to talk with you? He becomes a jealous God when we put things before Him. All He wants is your time and attention, your acknowledgment. I look forward to my time with Him, as I have mentioned before. It sets my day before me to have an encounter with Him first. It puts me in the right mood, and even if things go badly that day, I can face that day with strength and boldness from the Lord. Go somewhere quiet – a prayer closet – alone in a room or in your car, wherever your place is. Be still and listen for the voice of the Lord. He is there. He only needs us to slow down and be quiet. Allow Him to reveal what He has for you.

PRAYER:

My Lord, help us today to be still and quiet to hear Your voice. May we make time in our day to seek Your face. Give us a yearning for Your word and voice every single day. Thank You. In Your name, Jesus, Amen.

About the Author

Jessica McCormack is from a small town called Mansfield, Ohio. She is happily married to Zach and they have three amazing children. Jessica has been in a few different ministries over the years. Jessica and her husband have served as Youth Pastors in Children's Ministry, Drama Ministry and currently in Music Ministry and Praise and Worship. She has a passion for helping and encouraging others. Her vision is to reach out to those hurting and winning souls for God's Kingdom.

Index

A

anger, 3, 40, 52, 60–62, 65
authority, 43–44, 53

B

battle, 26, 44, 50
bitterness, 3, 20
blessing, 9, 27, 59
blood, 2, 45
boldness, 15, 70, 73
bondage, 10, 27

C

change, 26, 33, 48–50
comfort, 3–7, 66–67

D

demons, 22–23, 26
depression, 25–26, 48
disappointment, 44
discernment, 53, 57, 69
distractions, 2, 32
dreams, 9, 71

F

failures, 44–45
faith, 9, 11–12, 39–41, 49, 69
family, 2–3, 61
fear, 5, 12, 15, 44
freedom, 23, 26
fruit, 35–36, 51

G

gifts, 18, 56–57, 59, 72

God, 1–2, 4–6, 8–13, 15–16, 18–27, 29–37, 39–42, 44–45, 47–50, 53, 55–58, 61–62, 64–73, 75
grief, 64–66
guilty, 19, 36

H

happiness, 2, 26, 61
heartache, 44
hearts, 9–10, 20–21, 24, 29–30, 32, 41, 48–49, 52–53, 61, 64, 66, 69, 73
   broken, 2–3, 6, 13–16, 19, 30, 32, 41, 48–49, 51, 58, 62, 66, 69
Holy, 57
human nature, 60

I

idols, 19–20

K

Kingdom, 3, 70, 75

L

love, agape, 16

M

marriage, 26, 49–50
miracles, 21, 33, 50, 56
mountains, 12, 52

P

pain, 65–66
paths, 27, 38
patience, 39–41
peace, 6, 30–31, 50, 61–62, 66–67
power, 44, 47–48, 51
prayer closet, 73
prayer life, 31–32
prayer time, 32
praying, 23, 36
promise, 5, 32, 40, 67
prophecies, 14, 56

R

repent, 22, 72

S

salvation, 68, 70
sinners, 16, 22, 70
souls, 10, 20, 23, 70
strength, 6, 30, 36–37, 73

T

temptation, 24, 34, 36–38
testimony, 70, 72
tongues, 14, 51–52, 56–57
trust, 5, 12, 41–42

U

unworthy, 9–10

W

wisdom, 6, 53, 57–58
worry, 19, 44
worship, 18–19, 21

CPSIA information can be obtained
at www.ICGtesting.com
Printed in the USA
FSHW010342070720